DOWN MEMORY LANE

A TIME CAPSULE OF MALAYSIAN PLANTATION DAYS

VEERASAMY RENGAN

ISBN 979-8-89610-387-5

This book is dedicated to my family and to all my teachers.

Contents

Contents

Editorial Preface

In the heart of every memory lies a story, and in the pages of **'Down Memory Lane'**, Veerasamy Rengan masterfully weaves together the vibrant tapestry of his childhood, living amidst the green expanses of a Malaysian rubber plantation. This book is more than a memoir; it is a gateway to an era of simple joys, close-knit communities, and the enduring spirit of humanity thriving in harmony with nature.

From the gentle hum of early morning broadcasts awakening the plantation to the joyous laughter of children playing under a tropical sky, Veerasamy invites readers to walk alongside him through the vivid recollections of his formative years. His anecdotes of school days, festive celebrations, and communal togetherness evoke a nostalgia that transcends generations, reminding us of the enduring beauty in life's simplicity.

This narrative is also a tribute to the unsung heroes of the past, to traditions lovingly preserved, and to the resilience of families who found contentment in the modest abundance of their surroundings. Each chapter pulses with life, offering insights into the cultural heritage, daily routines, and personal milestones that shaped Veerasamy's journey from the rural estate to urban life.

As you embark on this journey, prepare to be inspired by the universal themes of love, perseverance, and community. Whether you are reliving your own cherished memories or discovering the echoes of a bygone era, this book promises to stir your soul and rekindle an appreciation for the stories that define us.

Welcome to **'Down Memory Lane'**—where every page is a step back in time, and every story is a celebration of life's timeless wonders.

–Dr. Chanthiran Veerasamy R.

– Kalai Selviy Veerasamy R.

Sunrise at the Estate: Memoirs of Malaysian Heritage

This short autobiography of my childhood memories is not only dear to me but to many who would like to re-enact and share these vivid and beautiful moments during their tender age while thinking about them when they have reached their twilight years.

I began my early childhood in the rural, green, and natural surroundings of a latex plantation company. The seven years of childhood from the age of five to about twelve, which I spent here until my transition from a rural to an urban life, was truly memorable when I recall the happy moments and memories during this childhood phase in my life.

Chapter 1
The Sunrise

The Sun was still in the far eastern corner of the dim skyline. Not long, it would be rising above the horizon, spreading its beautiful reddish-orange coloured rays over the sleepy rubber plantation. The night before had been very quiet except for the incessant sounds made by the noisy crickets and the occasional hoots made by the nocturnal owls. They had trespassed from the rubber plantation, closely bordering the living quarters of the plantation employees.

The time showed six in the morning. One could hear the roosters crowing at short intervals in their coops, here and there, as though trying to wake up the residents of the Estate. The people here usually got up quite early in the morning. In the early days, though normal radio broadcasts would start only as late as around four o'clock in the evening, there were special early morning short broadcasts in Tamil around six o'clock. These radio broadcasts were especially brought to the early birds, such as the plantation estate folks, who needed to attend to their duties in the early morning hours. These people would be entertained by listening to songs and news while doing their work before attending to their daily jobs in the estate.

The lady folks, especially, had to do a few chores. First, they had to prepare their school-going children to be ready for school. Next, the breakfast had to be prepared for their families. Sometimes, they prepare their own lunch boxes to take along with them. If the parents had small children, they left them at the crèche before beginning their duties in the Estate. The caretakers were all from the estate and were employed by the management. So, the parents did not worry much about leaving their children at the crèche.

There were not many job disciplines created by Estate management. Since the production of latex was of primary importance, being the only main resource and business of the Estate owners, most of the jobs were closely related to producing latex as the raw material. The latex tapped from the rubber trees in the plantation was processed into rubber sheets, dried and packed into bales for export at the Estate factories. As such, most of the people in the Estate were either employed at the rubber plantation or at the factory sites where the latex was processed.

The Estate management had a responsibility towards the welfare of its employees and staff. So, some of the employees were assigned to look after the well-being and health of the people. They were the sanitary service providers. They were responsible for maintaining the cleanliness of the living areas of the people, keeping them free of diseases.

Besides the above group of employees, the Estate also employed other staff like security guards, factory technicians, drivers, and clinic attendants. Most of the above preparatory activities of the employees were all done in the early or late dawn of the cool morning, before reporting for their duties just before daylight.

By seven o'clock in the morning, most of the Estate employees, especially at the field and factory sites, would have begun to attend to their duties, except for the clerical staff and school teachers who started theirs a little later, around eight o'clock. The Sun had now come up, slowly rising in the east. The day had begun its tireless journey. The daylight had gradually brought the whole rubber plantation in full view with all its natural splendour against the backdrop of the distant hills and the luxuriant rainforests.

Chapter 2
Joining School

The rubber plantation, or the rubber estate, as people usually referred to, was a European Latex Company. It was situated on the fringes of Kajang, a quiet town then. The estate was spread across a few acres of agricultural land. It was considerably large and was divided into two divisions, the East and West. Our family of six lived in the West, known as the Western Division.

It was quite a sustainable and self-sufficient estate with a generous living area for the estate residents and equipped with basic amenities such as electricity and water, though the supplies were restricted to specified time periods. It was also housed with other facilities like a school, a clinic, a Hindu temple, and a standard football field. In addition to these, it had an assembly hall where film shows, concerts, and estate committee meetings were held. The residents of the estate, I must say, did not lack the basic facilities needed for their day-to-day living.

It was in the mid-fifties when I first went to school at the age of five. The school, a Tamil school in the Estate, was a modest structure. It was enclosed with outer walls of zinc sheets at the bottom half and a two by two (inches) wire mesh at the top half. It had a corrugated zinc roofing. People standing outside of the school could clearly see the classrooms and students inside.

My two elder sisters had already joined the school before me, while my brother and I were left behind at home. My eldest sister was six years older than me, while my second sister was three years older. I felt envious when both my sisters went to school together. I started pestering my mother to send me to school, too.

One day, my mother told me that I could follow my sisters to school. I was on cloud nine, overjoyed to hear this. On the morning of my first day in school, I literally ran to school, grasping the graphite slate and lead pencil which my father had bought for me the day before. The slate and the lead pencil were the school stationery of the times for a beginner. These items are not heard of anymore, and frankly speaking, we could say they were memorable souvenirs that were worthwhile to keep in our house showcase for remembrance. Incidentally, students were allowed to use exercise books and pencils when they reached the third standard.

The school was a mixed school with boys and girls studying together. The students ranged from the ages of five to twelve, from pre-standard one classes to standard six. The students did not need to wear school uniforms, but the parents usually made sure their children went attired decently and neatly to school. The teachers, too, taught the students the importance of good personal hygiene. I still remember when they did spot-checks on students' fingernails to see if they kept theirs short and neat.

Those days, the highest class you could reach in a Tamil school was standard seven. To continue the seventh standard, the interested students had to attend lessons conducted by the government Tamil school in the nearby town, Kajang. After this, they would be trained to become Tamil school teachers. When I was studying at the school, one of the teachers, Mr Sundaram, was an old boy of the school.

Chapter 3
My First Day in School

The Estate management had allocated quite a large area for the Tamil school. There was no provision for a school field inside the school compound because the Estate football field was just adjacent to the school. All outdoor co-curricular activities, Physical Education classes, and the School Sports Day were all held here.

As such, the school had quite a sizeable compound around the school building. They could afford to have green vegetable and flowering gardens. When you pass by the short passageway from the main school gate to the entrance of the school building, you can see both sides of the passageway lined up with colourful flowering plants and blooms. There were the white daisies, the red roses, and the tall sunflower plants with large yellow flowers. As you reached the doorway, you would find the large Bougainvillea plants with bunched-up purple flowers creeping and spreading on one side of the building. In the cool early morning hours, the flowers of different types and colours gave a colourful front appearance to the school. Along the side fences of the school, you could also see clumps of leafy canna plants with pretty blooms of red and yellow flowers.

The school would start at seven-thirty in the morning. Those students who had come to school before this time would spend their time doing small jobs in the vegetable garden around the school. On the first day of school, I, too, was instructed by the school head boy to join some others to do the weeding for the vegetable beds. For me, the task was not a new experience, as I always followed my father to our own garden on the Estate. I really enjoyed that morning gardening and feeling the wet soil in my hands.

At seven-thirty in the morning, the head boy rang the handbell, which was the only timekeeper of the school, indicating the starting, recess, and finishing times of the school. By now, we all had washed up and had gone into the classrooms. The strength of the school was that it had only about sixty students. There were three teachers; Mr Joseph was the headmaster, assisted by Mr Kasipillay and Mr Sundaram.

I was seated in the classroom. Shortly after, my two sisters gave me some encouragement, which I really did not need because the presence of my sisters in the school gave me a lot of confidence and courage. A little later, the teacher, Mr Kasipillay, came into the classroom. He spoke to me for a while and noted my name in the class register. Then he gave some instructions to the class monitor, who took me outside beside the enclosing zinc wall. It was not noon yet, so the place was quite shady. I saw a corrugated zinc sheet covered with very fine sand. The monitor showed me how to write the Tamil vowel letters on sand using his forefinger. Then he guided my hand and asked me to do the same with mine. What a novel way of learning to write! No hassle at all, and fun too. After a few days of practising, I started using the graphite slate and lead pencil to learn to write the Tamil letters.

The medium of teaching for all the subjects was solely in Tamil. The students learned the 3Rs: Reading, Writing, and Arithmetic up to the second standard. When they reached the third standard, subjects like Geography, History, and Nature Studies were included up to the sixth standard.

To break the monotony of classroom studies, the local radio broadcasting stations broadcast special school programmes at specific times and days every week. The school did not have a radio. At that time, having a radio was partly a luxury. So, a tall wooden mast inside the school garden was erected, attached with a megaphone-like field speaker overlooking the school. It was wired to a radio in the Estate chief clerk's house close by, across the road in front of the school.

The radio programmes, usually, had nothing to do with the subjects taught in school. On the contrary, they were all entertaining dramatic stories and songs from Tamil folklores, fairy tales, and moral stories. The twenty or twenty-five-minute programmes were very enjoyable to the students, and they looked forward to the radio broadcasts every week. Later, when I was studying in an English primary school, the students there also had similar radio programmes but in English.

The allocation of Tamil schools in rubber plantations by various latex companies in the country has served a good purpose in making the children of the plantation employees literate and as a good first step in formal education in their lives.

Many of them grew up educated in the Tamil language, and some of them have become popular radio and TV news readers and announcers. Others have made a name for themselves as teachers, writers, journalists, and even orators.

Chapter 4
At the National English School

I was studying in the Estate Tamil School for about two years. When I reached the third standard, I switched to using a normal exercise book and a pencil, instead of a slate and a lead pencil. I felt very happy about the 'graduation', having a new feeling of using an exercise book and a pencil for the first time to write in the classroom after two years.

At the age of seven, my father decided to send me to the National English School in the nearby Kajang Town. I had to attend standard one class in the afternoon session. Prior to joining this school, my father took me to the school for an Assessment Test. Those days, students were always graded and streamed into classes ranging from A to C or D according to their progress marks or merits. Therefore, even before going to school, I had to sit for this test and be graded.

I was asked to sit in the classroom with some other students. To me, the school itself looked awesome. It was about three times as big as the Estate Tamil School. The classrooms were very spacious, with each having two doors on one side and a complete row of glass shutters on the opposite side.

There was a big rectangular blackboard fixed to the front wall of the classroom. The single-storey school building with a few rows was built with brick walls and asbestos roofing.

When the Assessment Test began, a teacher attended to each student. An Indian teacher was assigned to me. He hardly spoke any word of Tamil to me, neither could I speak any word of English. There was certainly a barrier in communication as well as language between us. Since I had two years of schooling at the Tamil school in the Estate, I was quite at ease with the teacher.

The test itself had something to do with the IQ (Intelligence Quotient) of the students, I suppose. He spoke in English and demonstrated to me what I should do. There were no words or sentences on the test papers except for coloured shapes and figures. It was all about matching suitable colours and shapes in varied forms. Though he spoke in English, I understood his gestures fairly well. I just needed to show the answers with my hand. During the short test, the teacher said 'good' and 'very good' many times in response to my answers. I assumed I did quite well. Finally, when the school reopened for the new session, I was admitted to the first class, Standard 1A.

I quite enjoyed the Tamil schooling and at the same time was very excited to have joined the English school in town. So, I decided to attend the Tamil school in the morning and the English school in the afternoon. Both my parents freely agreed to this arrangement. I would leave the Tamil school a little early and prepare myself to go to the other school in town in the afternoon. It was a full day for me when I came back from school in the evening.

It was sad to say that attending two schools at a time came to an end when the English school switched to the morning session for the next half of the year. That ended my Tamil education for me. Many years later, when I was in Form Four Secondary School, I had a chance again to continue learning the Tamil language in the P.O.L (Pupils' Own Language) class. The teacher who taught us encouraged the class to take up the subject and sit for the Tamil Paper in the Senior Cambridge School Certificate Examination. Having a strong liking for the language even during early childhood, I did a lot of self-study to prepare for the paper. A year later, I sat for the Tamil language Paper and managed to pass with good grades. My early Tamil schooling in the Estate must have made a strong impact on my Tamil language knowledge. Thanks to my teachers.

Chapter 5
Gratitude for a Mother

The English school in town was a big contrast to the rural Estate Tamil School. First, unlike the mixed Tamil school, it was wholly a Boys' School. Everything was formal and disciplined here. Next, students had to be in full uniform: short-sleeved white shirts, polished canvas shoes with white socks and black shorts. A student must at all times wear the school badge on his left shirt pocket. He could be sent to the detention class if he did not wear it to school.

My mother took care of me so that I could go to school on time, attired neatly and in uniform. She had some English education together with her younger sister when her family was living in Kuala Lumpur during the colonial days. My grandfather was working as a cook for a British administrator's family there. The lady of the house was of a kind nature and sent both sisters to a nearby convent, a boarding school, at her own expense. My mother was eight years old, and her sister was two years younger.

They studied at the convent for about five years until my grandfather decided to bring them back to the same Estate in which they had lived ever since. They continued their education in the same Estate Tamil School where my sisters and I studied. My mother reached the seventh standard, which was her final year at a Tamil school. Therefore, she already had some fair knowledge of English and was quite well-educated in Tamil. Naturally, she became my mentor and a dedicated tutor for me during my early school days.

She was very particular about my school uniform being white, clean, and neat. During that time, you could get soda pellets to laundry white clothing. She would use some of these pellets in a metal pail of water and boil my white uniform shirts inside the pail for about ten to twenty minutes. After washing and drying, the shirts would look as white as snow.

During the early 1950s, the electric iron was hardly heard of, and only irons heated by charcoal fire were used. We did not have one in our house, though my mother had a unique way of 'ironing' my uniform shirts and shorts. She would fold them neatly and place them underneath my straw mat on which I slept for the night. During my slumber, the uniform would be pressed by my body weight and warmth. The next morning, the uniform looked nearly as good as ironed without being much creased.

When I was in standard four, in the English school, our music teacher, Miss Phang, was preparing the school choir for the upcoming concert. I was selected to be in the choir, too. After the singing practice, we were seated on the floor while she briefed us on the procedures we should follow during the concert. She also touched on how we should be dressed up in full uniform. Suddenly, she selected a few students from the choir group and made them stand in a row in front of the other students.

I was one of the few students in the row. She told the other students the choir group should present themselves neatly in school uniform as the row of students standing in front. I was rather elated by her comments, and at the same time, I felt very proud of my mother, who saw to it that I went to school spick and span.

Besides caring for my school uniform and sending me to school clean and neat, my mother would also send me off to school with healthy breakfast meals. Normally, I would not have time to have breakfast in the morning. So, she would prepare a take-away breakfast in a tiffin box, which I would eat from during recess time, apart from the drinks and titbits that I bought at the school canteen.

The simple breakfast meals she made were prepared quite fast. She would make them from easily available grains like rice, green peas, or brown chickpeas. She would soak these beans overnight until the next morning; after that, they were boiled to be cooked, and the water strained out dry. A little coconut oil was heated in a frying pan with added ingredients of sliced onions, one or two pieces of cut red dried chillies, and fried with some mustard seeds and a little salt for taste until they had become slightly brown. Next, the cooked peas were mixed together and fried. A dish of fragrant and tasty green peas or brown chickpeas was ready in a jiffy. Fried cooked rice was also prepared fast using the same recipe. Sometimes, she would prepare 'thosai', a pancake, which also would not take much time to make. Rice and black gram dhal were soaked together for a few hours in water and ground into a thick, milky flour mixture. It was left overnight to be fermented. The next morning, a little salt was added to the mixture. A big spoonful of the frothy flour mixture was spread out thin over a heated flat pan. Some pure gingelly oil was sprinkled over the 'thosai' being cooked, and it was turned over once, using the flattened end of a ladle before being removed from the pan. Pieces of crispy golden brown 'thosai' could be prepared in a matter of few minutes.

I did not think much of these morning breakfast meals my mother prepared then, though I liked them very much. But years later, I realised they were, as a matter of fact, very healthy foods, indeed. Besides the above dishes, there was one more similar breakfast meal popular among the lady folks of the Estate. It was the 'uppuma', made of roasted par-boiled rice, which my mother used to make quite often. It was very tasty, too. It was prepared by roasting the light brown rice in a heated frying pan and then coarsely ground using a granite grinder ('ammi') and keeping it aside. A little coconut oil was heated in the frying pan, and the same ingredients (dried chillies, sliced onions, and mustard seeds) were added to the oil to prepare fried peas and rice. The ingredients were topped up with grated coconut shavings and a few strands of curry leaves, and the whole mixture fried till light brown. Water was added to about half-full of the pan and brought to boil. Enough sugar and salt were added to the boiling mixtures. Subsequently, the roasted rice set aside was slowly added into the boiling mixture and turned over uniformly with a ladle until it became porous, loose and separated. When cooled, a simple, brownish-looking, delicious breakfast meal was ready to be served.

All these breakfast meals, though they looked simple, were rich in nutrition. The fermented 'thosai' was rich in carbohydrates and vitamin B. Peas and rice were good sources of plant protein and carbohydrates. It was a wonder how the women of the yester years prepared these foods for their children by just following the practices handed down to them by their predecessors, perhaps without even knowing the rich nutritive values of the delightful foods prepared by them.

Chapter 6
The School Concert

Our school, the National Primary English school, used to have the school concert annually. It was an important, or rather, a grand occasion for the school. The school concert was equally highlighted as the Annual Sports Day. For both the school events, teachers, parents, and VIP guests would be invited together, making these two yearly occasions successful and memorable for the students.

At that time, I was still living with my family on the Estate, while my father was already employed at the hospital in Kajang Town. I was in the fourth standard when I took part in the school concert. Nearly every class was supposed to present a performance on the stage for the concert. Each class would be presenting stage events like humorous sketches, traditional dances, chorus singing, and dramatic plays. The participants would be attired in suitable and colourful costumes, making the stage shows presentable and entertaining.

For the current year, our class teacher, Miss Yong, discussed the performance our class was supposed to give for the concert. Finally, after some discussion, we agreed to present the traditional 'tarian piring' dance. It was also known as the 'candle dance', as lighted candles on porcelain saucers were held by both hands of each dancer.

Our class teacher selected seven participants from the class to form the dance troupe. A leader was chosen from the dance troupe as he was quite well-informed about the dance. He used to perform this 'candle dance' in his home village functions. Subsequently, he was teaching us the various movements of the dance.

The dance itself needed some concentration and a sense of balance so that the porcelain saucers held by the performers would not slip from their outstretched palms. A small candle was lit in the middle part of each saucer by melting a little candle wax and attaching it to the saucer. The candle would get stuck to the saucer when the wax solidified after a while, making it firm and upright and remaining intact when the dancers swayed their hands from side to side, to and fro, or above their heads. The dance, in short, was a coordinated movement of the hands, legs, and head. Extra care was needed so that the candles remained lighted and would not fall off the saucers during the performance.

The arrangement of the seven dancers on the stage was quite simple. They were arranged in a V-shape, facing the audience, with the leader of the troupe in the middle of the V-formation. A metal ring worn on the forepart of the middle finger of each hand of the dancer was used to produce musical sounds when struck on the bottom of the porcelain saucer. The musical sounds were further backed up by the music played on the piano. Our music teacher, Miss Phang, very skilfully composed a tune for the dance to be played on the piano by just listening to the leader of our dance troupe humming the tune. We practised for about two weeks and a rehearsal was held for all the stage performances a day before the concert was to take place.

On the day of the concert, a classroom was allocated for the participants to prepare themselves before going on stage. A group of lady teachers was in charge of putting make-up and fixing the costumes in place for the students. They sent the students to the stage on time and in an orderly fashion according to the scheduled events.

The concert started around 7.30 pm in the evening in the school hall. The hall was full of parents, teachers, and invited guests. They enjoyed watching all the performances one after the other with a big applause at the end of each stage event. Our music teacher was one of the teachers in charge of the stage and also played the piano when needed. Our performance, 'the candle dance', stood out in the concert. We appeared on stage in uniform costumes. Only during our performance all the lights on the stage were switched off, and the stage was brightened by only lighted candles on the saucers held by the dance performers. The view on stage was certainly something different for the audience on the floor. The dance, accompanied by the musical tinkling sounds produced by the porcelain saucers, enhanced by the melodious tune played on the piano by our music teacher, and the performers rhythmically moving the lighted candles in uniform steps on the dim candle-lit stage, was a sight to behold for the audience.

The concert was over around 9:00 pm. My father had come to watch the concert. Meanwhile, my mother was waiting for me at my father's quarters, which was not very far from the school. She came over from the estate specially to enable me to attend the concert. My father took me home to his place on a bicycle. My mother was glad to see us home. Later, when we were having our dinner, my father told my mother about our class performance at the concert. She was pleased to know that it was quite impressive and well-received by the audience. She gave me an affectionate hug before I went to sleep.

Following our school concert, came the National Independence Day on the 31st August for that year. Annually, grand celebrations would be held at the Town Field organised by the Kajang Town Council. Various events from morning till late in the evening would be held. During the night, stage performances would be held in the Town Field while the night sky would be brightened up by a colourful display of fireworks.

Our teacher, Miss Yong, announced to us that our 'candle dance' troupe was invited to perform on stage at the Town Field during the night of Independence Day. Our class performance must have impressed some dignitaries who were present on our school concert day.

Chapter 7
Simple Entertainment

The Indians living in the Estate were ardent cinema-goers. They were mostly fans of those days' popular Tamil film stars, MGR and Shivaji. Adjacent to the Estate, in Kajang Town, about one-and-a-half kilometres away, there were two cinema halls, the Sun Cinema and the National Theatre.

The employees in the Estate were paid wages twice every month by the Estate management. An advance payment in the middle of the month and the balance of salary at the end. Those were the times when Tamil films were shown in the two theatres, and the people could afford to go for a film show. My father, though not every month, would treat our family to film shows, not joining himself. He would rather prefer to stay home chewing betel leaves and chatting with his relative who lived a few houses away from ours. There were two private car owners in the Estate, and they would ply the Estate folks between the theatres and the Estate. As such, people would even go for the night shows. Some would prefer to walk the distance to the theatres during the daytime, as they were not very far from the Estate.

For people in the Estate, cinema shows were a simple entertainment outlet where they could spend a few hours happily at the theatre. Tamil films were rather long-winded and could last about three hours. Tamil films always depicted good morals, showing that the laws of justice would finally prevail over evil deeds. Even the theme songs in the films were motivating and were written about life philosophies and ideas. On the whole, Tamil film shows for the Estate folks were good family entertainment to pass the time.

Apart from going to watch shows in the town, the Estate folks got to watch film shows on the Estate itself. An appointed committee would be formed in the Estate to collect subscriptions for the films to be shown. They would be brought to them by mobile film companies. They were shown in an open-air theatre at night on the Estate football field. The film operators would erect a screen in the field. A projector using 16 mm films would be projected on the screen, unlike the 32 mm films shown on large screens at the two theatres in town. They used their generators to power their projectors.

The Estate folks would get a chance to see at least a show every month. If there were to be a film show at night, news would spread like wildfire from house to house. Everyone would be talking about the show at the tea-shop, barber's salon or even under the rain trees where youths would be hanging around chatting. Young girls at the water-tap stands, washing their clothes and fetching water for their cooking, would also be seen talking about the film to be shown at night.

The mobile van bringing the films would arrive early, around six o'clock in the evening, with children welcoming the van with shouts of joy. The film operators would make use of the daylight to put up the screen, set the projector, and test the speaker box and the generator to make sure they were in working condition. Around seven o'clock, they would start showing trailers before the main film show, which would be shown around eight o'clock.

Meanwhile, you could see throngs of people, young and old, carrying their own chairs, small benches, and straw mats heading towards the field from their houses. The lower management staff, like the field conductors and supervisors, would also join in to watch the film show.

The show normally would end around ten o'clock at night. Since the next day would usually be a Sunday, a holiday for the estate employees, they would not mind getting up late to start their day.

Chapter 8
Entertaining Stage Dramas

Apart from the entertaining cinema shows in the nearby town theatres and the mobile cinema shows in the Estate itself, the people in the Estate also got to watch and enjoy stage plays. These were brought to them and presented by small-time drama troupes. They depicted story classics from Indian mythologies, which were abundant in folklore, poetry, songs, and old-time yarns.

The scriptwriters of the plays did not need to come up with new storylines or ideas for the subject matters of their stage shows, which were, more or less, ready-made for them. People of those days were quite enchanted by stories from big epic classics like the 'Mahabharata' or the 'Ramayana'. Even the younger generations in the Estate knew of these story classics as they were told by word of mouth by their parents, grandparents or the elders from the Estate during storytelling sessions. Listening to these types of tales was an interesting pastime for the children of the yesteryears.

I, too, used to pester my mother for bedtime stories. My mother was an avid reader, and she had a 'library' of stories to tell. Tamil textbooks used in the Estate Tamil schools at the time also consisted of interesting anecdotes of the classics. As such, people, young and old alike, were quite well-informed about these classical tales. They appreciated and enjoyed watching classical plays brought to them live on-stage dramas, which were in a different perspective in contrast to the projected movies on screens.

There were not many stage-performing troupes around at that time. Looking at their well-performed shows, one could guess they were experienced actors and had performed on many stages before. The drama troupes usually come in small numbers, with about ten artists in each group and different types of paraphernalia, which included musical instruments, brightly coloured costumes, and other necessary stage tools and accessories.

The musical instruments were quite simple, too. They consisted of the main harmonium, a box-like musical wind instrument with a keyboard played like a piano, the drum 'mridangam', a hollow wooden frame open at both ends which were circular and covered with stretched leather membranes producing drumming sounds when hit with both hands. The supporting 'jalra', a two-piece brass cymbals disc, could be hit together to produce loud and sharp musical sounds.

The Estate had a committee in charge of stage and cinema shows. The drama troupe would get permission from the head of the committee to allow them to perform. Sometimes, they needed more than a day for their stage performances. The all-male troupe would be allowed to be put up at the Estate Temple building. In those days, the female roles in the plays were acted by males wearing female stage costumes, impersonating female characters.

The temporary stage with the raised platform was put up at the front portion on one side of the verandah of the bread shop in the estate. The scenes in the play, no doubt, would follow the storyline of the classics. The different scenes would be depicted by the different rolled-up backdrops: a royal scene at the palace, a sorrowful tragic scene at the cemetery, a happy duet scene by a prince and his sweetheart at the flower garden or a homely peasant with his happy family in a simple cottage. The rolled-up backdrops would be hidden at the backstage, hung one after the other. They would be rolled down at suitable times according to the different scenes.

The drama would start around seven-thirty at night when most of the people would have returned from work and have finished their house chores. Before the curtain was raised for the first scene of the play, the buffoon or the clown would appear on stage to keep the audience occupied with his funny jokes and antics while the first scene was being set up behind the curtain. When it was ready, the curtain would go up, followed by a big applause by the crowd. The clown would appear for a short while like this each time during an intermission for a change of scene.

With the different types of colourful costumes for the casts of the 'dewas', the demons, and the ordinary characters from the different rungs of the social ladder, it would be eye-catching to watch simultaneously the actors reciting eloquently the story dialogues, the background playback songs by the stage singers, and the supporting musical band, all done in tune systematically for the show.

Facilities like the PA system were not easily available then, not to speak of electrical power. The lack of a PA system was made up by the loud, robust voices of the musicians, who displayed their outstanding eloquence and clarity in reciting the dialogue lines. Thus, the message and the flow of the story would reach the audience audibly and clearly. Furthermore, the people would be seated on the ground quite close to the raised stage while the old folks would be seated on chairs at the back. A lot of youngsters would be standing around watching the play. The lighting system was also overcome when there was no electricity. A couple of portable gaslights hung on either side of the small stage were quite sufficient to make the stage bright.

The play would come to an end at one point in time to be continued, sometimes the next day. During the play and also at the end, there were many well-wishers donating cash and in-kind towards the coffers of the drama troupe. I had even seen some overseers in the Estate presenting gold rings to stage performers and members of the musical band who had performed remarkably well.

Chapter 9

Heyday for Petty Traders and Pedlars

When it was a red-letter day for the Estate employees receiving their advance or their salaries, it was also a heyday for small-time petty traders and pedlars. During these times, just outside the main entrance gate to the factory office, you could see quite a number of hawkers and traders exhibiting and peddling their wares, both food and other items for sale.

Normally, the employees of the Estate would be given an early break from their jobs. The dispensing of the salary payments to the employees would start around two o'clock in the afternoon, by which time they would have returned from their respective places of duty. They would wash up, dress themselves in clean clothes, and crowd around the office with happy, cheerful faces, waiting to receive their salaries. While waiting, they could be seen busily chatting with each other but at the same time being cautious not to annoy the manager and the office clerks at the table giving out their pay by not being too noisy.

The men, women, and youths of the Estate would make a cheerful and happy lot in front of the busy main office. The traders and hawkers in front of the factory entrance outside enhanced the busy and lively atmosphere of the place. Among the traders was the noticeable ice cream seller ringing his hand bell, trying to catch the attention of the children around. In another corner, you could see the balloon seller holding a bunch of strings with colourful balloons floating in the air. On a hot day, the ice cream seller would become quite busy selling his tasty and mouth-watering ice creams from his aluminium container box on his bicycle carrier.

Most of the traders and hawkers had come from the surrounding areas of the Estate, but you could also see some local Estate residents taking time off to make some quick money selling, especially food items like the 'vadai' which were flattened fried traditional titbits. They were of two types: one prepared from black gram dhal and the other from chickpea dhal. Both were spicy, the former with green chillies and onions, while the latter was made quite hot and spicy with added ground red dry chilli paste.

Another popular hawker was the 'chendol' seller, coming from the outskirts of Kajang Town on his tricycle cart. On his cart, he kept an enamel pot of 'chendol' already mixed from his house with coconut milk, green-coloured noodles, and brown sugar syrup, flavoured by an aromatic extract of pandan leaves. He would dispense this into small China bowls for his customers, topped up with finely grated ice. Though the ingredients for the 'chendol' looked simple on sight, he certainly would have a secret recipe to make it crowd-pulling.

Besides these traders who stationed themselves at one place temporarily to do their business, there were the mobile ones who went selling their wares on foot, from house to house in the Estate. One such trader was the clothes seller. He would sit in front of one of the houses and open his bundle of clothes to display. You would immediately see a small crowd of ladies around him. He normally sold sarongs for men and women for easy wear. A sarong was a long strip of cotton cloth colourfully patterned and worn around the hip. His merchandise also included rolls of cloth material which he would cut off for his customers using a pair of sharp scissors and a measuring yardstick. He hardly sold ready-made materials.

There was another mobile trader who would go house rounds on foot. He was the stone mason who would be much looked for by the Estate residents, as most of them had stone grinders in their houses. A stone grinder, or the 'ammi' as known in the Estate, was a useful tool for grinding dry red chillies for their curry when cooking. It was in the form of a granite stone tablet, having a rough surface area measuring about (11 by 18) inches and a height of 3 inches. It came together with a granite stone roller about 13 inches in length and a circumference of 12 inches. The roller was slightly tapered at both ends so that it was comfortably held by the hands to move to and fro repeatedly over the rough surface of the tablet grinder. The roller was made extra smooth all around so that it moved freely over the tablet grinder to grind materials like dry red chillies. After frequent grinding, the rough surface of the tablet might become eroded and lose its roughness, thus becoming ineffective for grinding purposes.

The stone mason's job was to skilfully chip the tablet to restore its roughness. He carried with him a small bag in which he kept a hammer, a sharp pointed chisel, and a pair of goggles to protect his eyes from splinter chips when chipping. He also kept a piece of rag to wipe off the dust from chipped splinters. He made use of the hammer and the sharp pointed chisel for chipping. When the job was done, the tablet grinder would look neat with its surface restored. Even though the process of chipping looked simple, it needed skill and patience, as it was possible to chip off a big piece of the tablet's surface, damaging it.

The charges for the job, as I could remember, were quite inexpensive, probably two or three dollars. Now, this craft has slowly died off with the times, with very few people using the granite stone grinders. They have been gradually replaced by modern electrically operated machine grinders.

Chapter 10
The Bioscope Entertainer

"Come on, come on! Come and watch the bioscope." Those were the calls made by the bioscope showman when he came around the Estate after dusk when night fell. He would come about seven o'clock at night carrying his bioscope show box on his bicycle carrier.

Children nowadays might not know or have seen the bioscope show which the showman had brought to the Estate. It was a kind of simple cinematography with a series of still photographic picture images on a rolled paper film. The pictures were usually of popular cinema artists or community and national personalities. They also consisted of various pictures of famous places and animals like the Taj Mahal, deer, parrots, and peacocks. The bioscope mainly attracts Estate children and teenagers.

As far as I can remember, the bioscope was similar to an enclosed metal box, rectangular in shape, measuring about 17 inches by 29 inches in width and length, respectively. The box was about a foot in height. Inside the box, there was, as already mentioned, a rolled paper film about 4 inches in height, consisting of photographs of images. The roll of paper film strip was fixed to a turning rod on the right side of the box with the handle lever for turning on top of the enclosed box. A similar turning rod was fixed on the left. One end of the rolled strip of paper film on the right was joined to the turning rod on the left. The strip of paper film, thus connected, could be moved by the handle levers attached to the rods from right to left or vice versa.

There were two big circular magnifying glasses fixed on either side in front of the box. The glasses were focused onto the movable strip of pictures, so that two viewers at a time could watch the show by placing their faces close to the glasses, seated on stools side by side. A lantern-lit inside the ventilated box gave light and brightness to the interior of the bioscope. When viewed through the magnifying glasses at night, the still pictures on the paper film produced a realistic cinematographic visual-effect view.

In the Estate, the empty space between two rows of houses was quite big enough for a crowd to gather around the bioscope showman. Under the starry and sometimes full moonlit sky, it would not be too dark for him to operate his show. Besides, the place would also be brightened by the lights from the rows of houses on either side. A viewer would be charged twenty cents per show, which might last for about ten minutes.

One would be wondering how still photographic pictures, watched by viewers, could be made interesting for them on a quiet night. On the contrary, the bioscope entertainer could make his show more than lively by his good showmanship with his self-created songs and dialogues. As he was singing and speaking to the crowd, he would move the roll of picture images one after the other for the viewers. At each change of picture, he would talk to the viewers about the picture they were watching. He would know the picture each viewer was watching through a small window beside him on top of the box.

He would find out their names from the people in the crowd and relate them in jovial and humorous commentaries, pulling them and the crowd into the show. There would be peals of laughter from the crowd around him, making the show entertaining. As backup music, he would use a rattle to tap on the metal bioscope box to match the tune of his songs.

These were some of the simple but happy moments the children and young people of the yesteryears in the Estate enjoyed. Nowadays, bioscope shows have become obsolete. It is rare to see a bioscope, except, maybe, in the oldies of Tamil movies. One would wonder about the dramatic and jet-fast changes that have come about in cinematography when you compare the bioscope with what you get to watch on television and other modern electronic gadgets.

Chapter 11
Deepavali

There were not many festive events in the Estate I lived in. Nevertheless, one of the occasions was worth mentioning. Namely, the Deepavali celebrations by the Hindus of the Estate were a grand festival. It is also known as the Festival of Lights, depicting the victory of good over evil.

The preparation of festival goodies, sweet as well as spicy, was an important aspect of the celebrations. The lady folks would start preparing them as early as one month ahead since they had to attend to their routine duties for the estate management and might not have enough time. So, they usually complete their household chores for the day and start preparing the flour and other essentials needed to make the festive goodies late in the evening. It would be a cooperative effort both by family members and neighbours. It was also a cheerful time for the lady folks to get together to share and show their goodwill and friendly neighbourliness. The happy mood would be further enhanced when the popular goodies of different types, namely, the 'murukku', 'omopodi', ghee balls and the like, were completed and safely stored in tins and bottles to be put aside for the big day.

It was not like now when women have quite an easy task preparing for Deepavali. Nowadays, the starting materials like the different types of flour are ready-made. They need only to be mixed with coconut milk or some other ingredients. On the other hand, women of the yesteryears prepared the flour in a tedious manner, using traditional utensils such as the wooden 'ural' and the stony 'thiruvakkal' for grinding and powdering into dry or wet flour.

The 'ural' consisted of two parts, both made of wood. A hollow receptacle was cut out from a heavy block of wood to contain the wet or dry grains. A straight, long, cylindrical piece of wood was used to pound into the hollow receptacle. It was held between both hands and repeatedly pounded up and down until the grain was powdered into flour. Both dry and wet flour were made this way. To make the job less tiring, two people would pound one after the other at the same time.

Another utensil was a type of grinder known as the 'thiruvakkal'. It consisted of two circular disc-like stony, heavy blocks, each a foot in diameter and half a foot in height. The top block was fixed with a short wooden handle at one edge for turning over the bottom block. The bottom block had a short wooden stud in the middle through which the top block, which also had a matching hollow in the middle, would be slotted into the bottom block. The roasted grain would then be slowly added into the hollow of the top block while being turned repeatedly in a circular motion with the handle. The resulting ground grain would be collected as flour at the sides of the bottom block. It was only used to produce dry flour.

Both the utensils, the 'ural' and the 'thiruvakkal', had become obsolete now, replaced by modern electrical blenders and grinders.

Although the preparations of flour were tedious and time-consuming, the lady folks of the Estate did them with cheer, pomp, and full of interest. Picture the sight of every household engaging itself late in the evening in the preparations and the sounds of merriment made by the happy laughter and chatter of the ladies, prolonging through the night.

On the auspicious morning of Deepavali, the children of the house would take oil baths, and the parents would follow suit after them. Before this, the lady of the house would have been very busy cooking throughout the night, preparing various types of food items for breakfast and also for the offerings of ancestral prayers.

After taking the oil bath, the children and parents would be in their usual attire. The head of the house would make preparations for the ceremonial prayers. The various types of curries, rice, fruits, and flowers would be offered for the prayers. During this time, all the new clothes bought for the family would be tinged with a dash of turmeric powder and be placed together to be blessed.

After the prayers, the whole family would sit together for a sumptuous breakfast of 'thosai', a soft-cooked pancake or 'idly', a soft steamed pudding. Both foods were prepared from soaked, fermented rice and black gram dhal blended together. They would make a tasty combination to be eaten with the curries. After breakfast, the children would begin excitedly wearing their new festival clothing. They would then receive blessings from family elders by bending down and touching their feet.

Breakfast would be followed by visiting guests, including the children and parents. This 'open house' would go on until late in the evening. During this time, you could see the whole house moving in a festive mood. The guests would be chatting and laughing with the family members, while helping themselves to the Deepavali treats.

During the night, the children would have a joyful time playing with firecrackers and coloured sparklers. The neighbourhood children would come together, making the occasion merrier. Parents, too, would join the fun.

Later in the night, the whole plantation estate would become quieter, except for the occasional bursts of firecrackers here and there. The whole family would retire to sleep, tired but happy with the satisfaction of having had a wonderful Deepavali celebration and longing for it again the following year.

Chapter 12
The Harvest Festival

The Harvest Festival or the 'Ponggal' was observed by most of the people in the estate. It is still being observed by Indians in Malaysia. It is celebrated on a grand scale by the farmers of India after harvesting the padi. It is usually celebrated for three days.

The Indians of those days in the Estate observed the festival for two days. The first day was the 'Surya Ponggal', which was the thanksgiving Day to the Universal Sun, while the second-day celebration was the 'Mattu Pongal', which was in recognition of the contribution given by the farm cows to the farmers. Cows helped to plough land, provided milk, and transported people and goods.

Normally, the two days were rest days for the employees in the Estate. Each household would be preparing for the occasion by buying the new 'ponggal panai', an earthenware clay pot to prepare the sweet rice. On the festival day, six new bricks were bought to set up the temporary enclosed brick stove in front of the house. Two stalks of sugar cane were put up on each side of the doorway of the house. The pot filled with fresh cow's milk was placed on the stove to be boiled just before sunrise, facing east. At sunrise, the whole family members would gather around the pot for the milk to be heated and boiled over the sides of the pot, frothing with bubbles. When this happened, you could hear the family members' shouts of 'ponggoloh ponggal'. At this time of the early morning, you could hear similar shouts inviting the Day from various corners of the Estate.

After the milk had boiled over and subsided into the pot, washed white rice, brown sugar, ghee-fried cashew nuts and raisins, and a little ghee would be added to make the mixture. Once the rice was done, some of it would be placed on a fresh banana leaf facing the east and the Sun. The head of the family would break open a coconut into halves to start the prayers, after which the sweet 'ponggal rice' was served to all the members of the family.

On the second day of the celebration, the service of the cows to the farmers would be highlighted as the 'mattu ponggal'. Unlike now, a lot of people in the estate owned cows. Keeping cattle was a secondary source of income, adding to their salaries from estate employment. The cows were kept in sheds away from the living quarters. Each owner of the cows was given a cubicle to house his cows.

My aunt, who was staying in the same estate, had about three milking cows. She obtained enough milk from the cows to sell to the customers in the estate in quarter bottles. She would collect the payment for her sales after the salary day in the estate.

Usually, all cows in the shed were herded daily by an appointed cowherd for grazing. They were brought back to the shed in the evening. But on this special day for the cows, all the cattle would remain in the shed. Grass for grazing would be brought to them.

My brother and I helped my aunt to decorate her cubicle shed by stringing and hanging weaved, yellow-coloured young coconut leaves. She had also put up sugar canes at the entrance of the cubicle. The cows were bathed in the shed itself. They were then decorated with flower garlands, tinkling bells, and milky-white conches around their necks.

Next, my aunt prepared the same sweet 'ponggal' rice in front of the shed, as she had done on the first day in her house. The sweet rice prepared was fed to all the cows in the cubicle shed. I was rather amused, thinking how the cows would have rejoiced over their special 'mattu ponggal' Day.

Chapter 13

A Scary Encounter

During the early days when the plantation settlements began, cement and bricks were hard to come by. People in the estate made their own stoves for cooking from mud clay obtained from the river. They made use of firewood from dead rubber trees as fuel.

I had seen my father making our cooking stove on the floor at the far end of the house veranda from mud clay he collected from the river nearby. He worked out skilfully with his hands two enclosed stoves side by side, leaving the front portion open for placing the firewood. The wet stoves would be left to air-dry for about two or three days. In due course of time, the clay would be baked by the heat produced during subsequent cooking and would be hardened after frequent use. They were as good as enclosed stoves made of bricks. He shaped the clay stoves appropriately to suit our kitchenware pots and pans. Later, when cement and bricks were available, people used enclosed stoves made of bricks and surfaced with cement.

Like the other people in the Estate, our family, too, collected and used firewood for our cooking. My father and elder sister would usually go to the nearby rubber plantation to collect the firewood. One of those days, my sister did not follow my father, but my younger brother and I followed him. I was nine years old then, and my younger brother was three years younger than me. It was about five o'clock in the evening when we reached the nearby rubber plantation to collect firewood. The place we went to was quiet, or rather, very hilly. We could see the Estate manager's bungalow at the hilltop.

In hilly areas, the rubber trees were planted on terraces from the bottom to the top. They formed a neat and orderly arrangement on the hill slopes. My father was somewhere in the middle of the hill collecting firewood. My brother and I climbed up the hill to get a better view of the bungalow at the top. After some time, we were quite high up the hill when my father asked us to come down and join him. It was then that I tried to stride down the hill. The terraces were not very far apart, so I took long strides to come down.

At first, I ran down clearing each terrace with my long strides. Suddenly, I realised I could not stop myself from running down the steep slope. I ran down terrace after terrace and each time gaining more and more speed like a car racing down a steep hill without brakes. When I reached the hill bottom at maximum speed, my good fortune helped me. I tripped over a twig and fell down on a heap of dried leaves. I was quite unscathed and got up by myself.

By this time, my father and brother had come down to help me. My father was shaken up but relieved that I was safe. The spot where I tripped over and fell was a cliff. Its edge was very near to where I came down on the ground. A few metres down the cliff edge below was a gravel road. Again, I would say, my good fortunes saved me from serious harm. I feared to imagine my fate if I had fallen off the cliff.

Chapter 14
The Football Field

The standard football field, not to be found even in urban areas, was a landmark to the Estate. I should say that the game of football must have been part of the culture in the Estate, which was established and managed by a European Latex Company, as already mentioned. Europeans were known to have a fervent interest in the game from those days. So much so, the football field with its wooden, white-washed goalposts on either end must have been there already when the rubber plantation company began its operations in the early years.

The grass in the soccer field was periodically cut short and trimmed by a diesel-operated lawn mower. The cut grass was swept clean, and the whole field would look like a huge level-green grassy plain. Since the field was a standard one, it occupied quite a large area in one corner of the Estate. It was situated some distance away from the living quarters of the Estate employees. The back and the right side of the field were bordered by rubber trees, which formed part of a plantation task. In front of the field was a gravel road that led to the manager's bungalow, which was far inside the plantation. Some distance away to the left side of the field was a row of houses occupied by the clinic hospital Assistant and the clerical staff.

The Estate always had a football team representing it. In the evenings, the field was seldom left vacant. There were always people practising football or exercising. During the evenings, the youth groups would form opposing teams among themselves and would be actively engaged in the game. During the weekend holidays, the school children had no school, so they would be in the field as early as eight o'clock in the morning playing football. Normally, they could not afford a leather-made football. So, they would use inflated rubber balls instead and play the game barefooted. The children showed such interest in the game.

The football team representing the Estate was formed by young and sturdy youths. Sometimes, married young men would also join the team. The team was fully supported and adopted by the Estate management. The standard footballs, boots, striped stockings, and jerseys for the team were all subsidised by the management, too. When the team, with its full gear, was engaged in a competitive game against another opposing team, it was a sight to behold with each team of players on both sides wearing their uniform-coloured jerseys. All the children in the Estate would come to the field to cheer up their home team. You could see a lot of excitement in the field until the game was over.

The team had its own captain and referee, who was an employee of the estate. Even though he was not a trained referee, he knew his job well, as he was a former goalkeeper for the Estate team. He was quite popular and controlled the matches well with his professional-like gestures and timely sharp blows of his whistle. Normally, very seldom competitive tournaments were arranged, but throughout the year, friendly games with neighbouring estates were frequently held.

The schoolchildren were quite influenced by the inherent football culture of the Estate. I was one of them captivated by it. I had an opportunity to bring out this trait in me, which I had acquired by playing football on the estate field. When I was in the sixth standard of studying in the English primary school in town, I was fortunate enough to be selected to wear the school jersey for the school football team. Thanks to the training and practices I had with my friends on the Estate soccer field.

Chapter 15

Sustainable and Self-sufficient

Coming to think of it, life in the Estate, I must say, was quite comfortable. We did not need to have a lot of cash in hand to make a living here.

Water, electricity and some other facilities were all given free by the Estate management. When both parents went to perform their daily duties in the Estate, the small children and babies were looked after in the crèche by 'ayahs' or Estate-employed caretakers. They were generally looked after well as the 'ayahs' lived in the same Estate, and they were known well by the parents.

As for the cleanliness, the surroundings in the Estate were well taken care of by the management, which was well-equipped with human resources. The drains and the common toilets were cleaned daily. The surrounding areas of the living quarters of the employees were also cleaned daily to remove litter and rubbish. Periodically, the living areas were sanitised by spraying disinfectant to control rodents, pests, mosquitoes, and other insects. The grass was cut when it was overgrown. The Estate, as a whole, gave a picture of tidiness and neatness.

If you were industrious, you could make a great living on the Estate. After the usual working hours, you could make good use of your free time. My father, who had green fingers, liked gardening. He owned two vegetable gardens and growing varieties of vegetables, namely, the long beans, four-angled beans, pointed okras, short beans, green chillies, and purple brinjals. Leafy vegetables like spinach, mustard leaves, fragrant curry leaves, and sour sorrel leaves were also grown. Fruits like bananas, papayas, and jackfruits were also obtained from his garden. During harvest time, the vegetables were always in excess. So, my father would tie them in bundles and send me on rounds using his bicycle to sell them to the residents of the Estate. Each bundle cost only thirty cents.

Keeping chickens was a favourite pastime for my father. He had a knack for carpentry and built an impressive chicken coop, complete with straw-filled boxes for the hens to lay eggs and also for roosting. When new chicks were hatched, he would feed the brood with broken rice mixed with mashed garlic and a little turmeric powder. He said feeding this way would keep the chicks from future infection with chicken diseases. Normally, we do not use chicken meat for our own consumption, except for eggs. He would rear the fowls until they were full-grown and sell them to the stall-keeper in the Kajang market just before Deepavali. The money obtained from the sales would help him cover his festival expenses.

Our family was fairly self-sufficient as far as farm products were concerned. We had enough eggs, chicken meat, fruits, and vegetables. My father went to the Kajang market only to buy things that he could not get from the estate, such as bean sprouts and soya-bean cakes (tofu). Sometimes, he bought fish and vegetables like cabbage and tomatoes or fruits like rambutans and mangosteen. Consequently, we would get almost everything for our daily needs from the Estate itself. It was not necessary to go to the town frequently to buy things.

A cooperative sundry store was managed by the Estate for the benefit of its employees. It had a full-time store clerk and a store assistant for packaging and dispensing. The employees in the Estate could open an account to buy things on credit to a certain limit. They were given small booklets in which their purchases would be recorded. The store clerk would also make similar records in his master record book for the Estate employees. Payments for things they buy will be deducted from their monthly pay.

Our family, too, made use of these facilities to buy our monthly provisions. As such, people in the Estate did not need to go to the town to buy their groceries.

Chapter 16
The Bread Shop

The bread shop in the Estate, next to the Cooperative Grocery Stores, was a very well-known and frequently visited place. It was situated just beside the main gravel road leading from the nearby town to the Estate. Directly in front were the enclosed office and factory areas. Immediately at the back were the rows of houses occupied by the Estate employees. Naturally, because of its strategic position, everyone had easy access to the shop.

The shop was owned by a Pakistani shopkeeper. He and his employees, who were his relatives, lived together in the shophouse. There was a large, attached bakery where the flour would be kneaded in bulk on a large table to make the dough for the bread. The main ingredients for the dough were quite simple substances like wheat flour, baking powder, and water. The dough was made into different shapes and sizes with added ingredients and given different names. It was prepared in the evening a day ahead before being baked the next morning. After being made ready, it was put into suitable trays: the slender long trays for the sugar cream and raisin bread, the rectangular trays for the full plain loaves, and the slotted trays for the round sugar and coconut buns.

The selling prices of the bread ranged from ten cents for buns to thirty cents for loaves. Breads were sold quite cheaply in those days.

The above breads were all homemade in the shop itself. A large kiln-like oven was built at the far back end of the shop. It had a spacious baking area enclosed all around with bricks and a square window-like opening in front. It was fixed with a removable shutter, which could be opened or closed. The bottom part of the window was at the same level as the floor base of the oven. As such, the trays of bread dough could be slid in or slid out through the window smoothly and easily. The two-foot square window was about four feet above the floor level of the shop.

The shop employees woke up very early in the morning, at about six o'clock. They needed about three persons working together to complete the baking process of the bread. First, the oven was heated up by burning a heap of firewood inside the oven until all the firewood was burnt out into ash and charcoal. By this time, the inside of the oven had become red hot. The ash and charcoal were then scraped out into a metal tray by using a scraper fixed to a long handle. The tray of hot ash and charcoal was quickly cleared off to the back of the shop and doused with water. Next, the oven was again cleaned with a mop of jute cloth tied to a long handle to clear off the remaining ash and pieces of charcoal.

After this, the metal trays containing the prepared dough were pushed and slid in through the window with a long handle. A flat piece of metal plate was fixed to one end of the handle on which the metal trays, a few at a time, were placed.

When all the trays of dough were neatly stacked and arranged inside the oven, the window of the oven would be closed with the shutter until the baking time was over. The trays of baked bread were then taken out through the window in the same way as they were put in. The oven would be left to cool down by itself. If you were standing nearby when the trays of baked bread were being taken out, you could smell the pleasant, rich aroma of freshly baked bread.

The scraping and cleaning of the oven, putting in the trays and taking them out after baking were all done timely and fast. The timing of baking was just as important as using a modern electrical oven to avoid the baking from being overdone or underdone. The baked breads would be sold directly from the bread shop.

In the evenings, when the Estate folks had already returned home from their duties, the bread baked in the morning would be sold to them fresh. One of the shop assistants would put the bread in a large round rattan basket covered with an aluminium hood. He would place the basket on a large carrier of his bicycle and go on rounds selling the bread from house to house in the Estate.

Every morning during school days, my friends and I would gather at the bread shop around six-thirty to wait for the car driver to pick us up for the English school in town. During the cold mornings, while we were waiting for him, we would go inside the shop to warm ourselves in front of the oven. The shop assistant would be busy preparing to bake the bread. They would allow us in as long as we kept a safe distance from the hot oven.

At that time, we might have been too young to appreciate or think much of these assistants in the shop or their jobs. But many years later, when we were living in a high-tech world with many conveniences, we used to wonder how those people of those days went about happily doing their daily routines without a care in the world. They could make do with whatever they had without the aid of any technology. How amazing of them!

The presence of the bread shop producing its own homemade bread was another classic example of the Estate's self-sufficiency. Its people did not need to depend on the commercially produced bread supply from the nearby town.

Chapter 17
Recycling: An Age-old Practice

We tend to think of recycling as a new trend, but the people in the Estate those days had been practising this without even knowing that they were actually recycling. There were a few simple recycling methods which they did in their everyday lives.

Those days, refrigerators were hardly heard of, even more rarely seen. Therefore, the Estate folks had many innovative ways of processing or storing food. One such method was the fermentation of leftover cooked rice. If there was excess cooked rice after the family had their dinner, fresh water would be used to immerse the cooked rice in a clay pot and kept covered overnight. The next morning, the fermented rice could be added with some salt, chopped onions, and one or two green chillies, which were also chopped. The rice would be hand-blended by squeezing it together with the added ingredients. A healthy, vitamin B-rich drink had already been prepared. It could be served as a refreshing drink for a tired farmer working in the field on a hot day.

During Deepavali celebrations, there would be an excess of mutton meat to go around. My father would join a group of friends to make an order for the meat. After sharing among them, each one would have more than enough meat to cook for the family. Sometimes, they would sell part of their shares to their friends. At other times, what they did was to preserve the meat for future use.

My father would do this by recycling the meat by first cutting it into small pieces. He would mix them with a fair amount of salt and turmeric powder mixed with a little water to make the mixture just wet. It was soaked for about an hour. Then, he would string the pieces of meat through a jute string and hang them outside under the Sun to dry during the day. A day of drying would not be sufficient. The string of meat would continue to be dried in the verandah of the house at night. This drying process could go on for a week or so until the pieces of meat become bone-dry. Next, he would unstring the pieces and store them tightly capped in a bottle. The pieces of dried meat could be added a few at a time whenever needed in cooking other dishes, even together with vegetables. The dried meat could easily last for about a month without getting spoiled.

We could find many uses for the different parts of the coconut tree. Some of its parts need not be discarded. They could be turned into useful recycled items. For example, the reed-like coconut leaves could be made into simple brooms.

The Estate folks made their own brooms. They collected the coconut leaves and shaved off the green leafy part, leaving the yellow hard main stem in each leaf. A handful of these thin stems tied together would make an excellent house broom. Some would even turn this into a small cottage industry for producing brooms for sale. You could say no house in the Estate was without this homemade broom.

My father used to make fine ladles from coconut shells. He would select a small or medium-sized half shell which had already been grated. The other half with eyes was not chosen because it was not suited to make a ladle. The cup-like shell was shaved off the husk both inside and outside until the shell became smooth all over. Then, two holes were made facing each other a little above the bottom of the shell. A short, slender wooden handle less than a foot long was selected. The half shell was fixed to one end of the handle, making it pass through the two holes tightly and snugly. The ladle thus made needed no other fixtures, and it was ready to be used.

The ladle was usually used to scoop cooked rice. Sometimes, my father would help make such ladles for his neighbours if they requested. As a matter of fact, it did not cost him much except his free time.

If recycling is the process of treating waste materials that have already been used so that they can be used again, upcycling is the process of reusing an item that is of the same or higher quality than its original. It requires only creativity and effort, unlike recycling, which may require energy or water to break down the materials. During most parts of the fifties in the last century, refrigerators were uncommon and rarely seen in the plantation estates. Maybe you could find them in the town in the coffee shops.

My father had a unique way of upcycling ordinary tap water into fridge-cool drinking water. He always used to keep water for drinking, covered in a large clay pot container similar to a large basin. It was kept in one corner of the room where we ate our meals.

The thick layer of clay surrounding the pot was a bad conductor of heat, so the warm room temperature had no effect at all on the stored water inside the container, thus keeping it cool. The latent heat of the water inside the container would be gradually lost due to slow evaporation, further cooling it.

On a hot day, we could get a drink of fridge-cool water from the clay pot. My father would replace the water every two or three days.

Chapter 18
Moving to Town

Our family lived in the Estate until I was eleven years old. Initially, my father was employed in the estate for some years, after which he was offered a government job as a general staff member at the hospital in Kajang. He continued staying with us in the Estate while cycling daily to work from the Estate to the town.

Meanwhile, he managed to obtain his living quarters in the town inside the hospital compound. Then one day he decided to move out his family from the Estate. It was just before the year 1960 when I was in the fifth standard.

At first, we were all saddened to move out and leave our long-time friends and neighbours. My mother was truly tearful. She had her education in the Estate, was brought up here, was married and started her own family here. Therefore, she had a big circle of friends and relatives in the Estate. Needless to say, she became very upset when she had to leave.

It was late in the evening one day. We packed up our household belongings onto a big lorry to be transported to our house in town. Our good neighbours were very helpful to pack up and transfer the things to the lorry. My father had already hired a private car in which our family followed the lorry bringing our things to town. For the last time, we bade goodbye to the happy moments, everlasting memories, good neighbours, trustworthy friends, and the lush, green rubber plantation for good.

We reached our new home in town within an hour, as the town was not too far from the Estate. The lorry attendants unloaded our things from the lorry briskly. Our new neighbour, who was my father's working colleague, also helped to move things inside the house.

The government quarters for general staff were not very big. It had a single bedroom, a kitchen, and a verandah which also served as the dining area. My father had already modified the verandah into another room with a door and a window. So, for the time being, we felt it was quite sufficient for our small family.

For me, it was not going to be so much of a dramatic change. The English school I was attending for the last four years was just beside the hospital Complex, my father's workplace. He used to meet me during recess time while I was living with my family in the Estate. Still, I felt sad leaving behind the wonderful time I had in the Estate. Surely, I would miss my friends there. The life and good times I had would stay memorable to me for a long time to come.

Every time the Sun rose, breaking the dawn of the morning into a bright and beautiful day, it also had to set in the evening at dusk, followed by the cool quiet night. For me, I would wake up the next day to another good morning and a new and different urban life in a completely new environment. Goodbye and thanks to the Estate I had been living for its simple joys, exciting moments, and sweet memories.

"A moment lasts all of a second, but the memory lives on forever."

9 798889 610387 5